HAL•LEONARD
INSTRUMENTAL
PLAY-ALONG

AUDIO ACCESS
INCLUDED

CLARINET
Piazzolla Tangos

To access audio visit:
www.halleonard.com/mylibrary

5908-7672-0516-8639

ISBN 978-1-4950-2840-3

BOOSEY & HAWKES

AN IMAGEM COMPANY

DISTRIBUTED BY

HAL•LEONARD®
CORPORATION
7777 W. BLUEMOUND RD. P.O. BOX 13819 MILWAUKEE, WI 53213

www.boosey.com
www.halleonard.com

AUSENCIAS
(The Absent)

CLARINET

ASTOR PIAZZOLLA

EL VIAJE
(The Voyage)

CLARINET

ASTOR PIAZZOLLA

Slower *rit.*

CHANSON DE LA NAISSANCE
(Song of the Birth)
from FAMILLE D'ARTISTES

CLARINET

ASTOR PIAZZOLLA

MILONGA
from A MIDSUMMER NIGHT'S DREAM

CLARINET

ASTOR PIAZZOLLA

LIBERTANGO

CLARINET

ASTOR PIAZZOLLA

LOS SUEÑOS
(Dreams)
from SUR

CLARINET

ASTOR PIAZZOLLA

mp

dim. **pp**

OBLIVION

Clarinet

ASTOR PIAZZOLLA

OUVERTURE
from FAMILLE D'ARTISTES

CLARINET

ASTOR PIAZZOLLA

SENSUEL
(Sensual)
from A MIDSUMMER NIGHT'S DREAM

CLARINET

ASTOR PIAZZOLLA

Moderate Tango

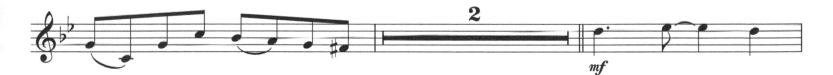

SENTIMENTAL
from FAMILLE D'ARTISTES

CLARINET

ASTOR PIAZZOLLA

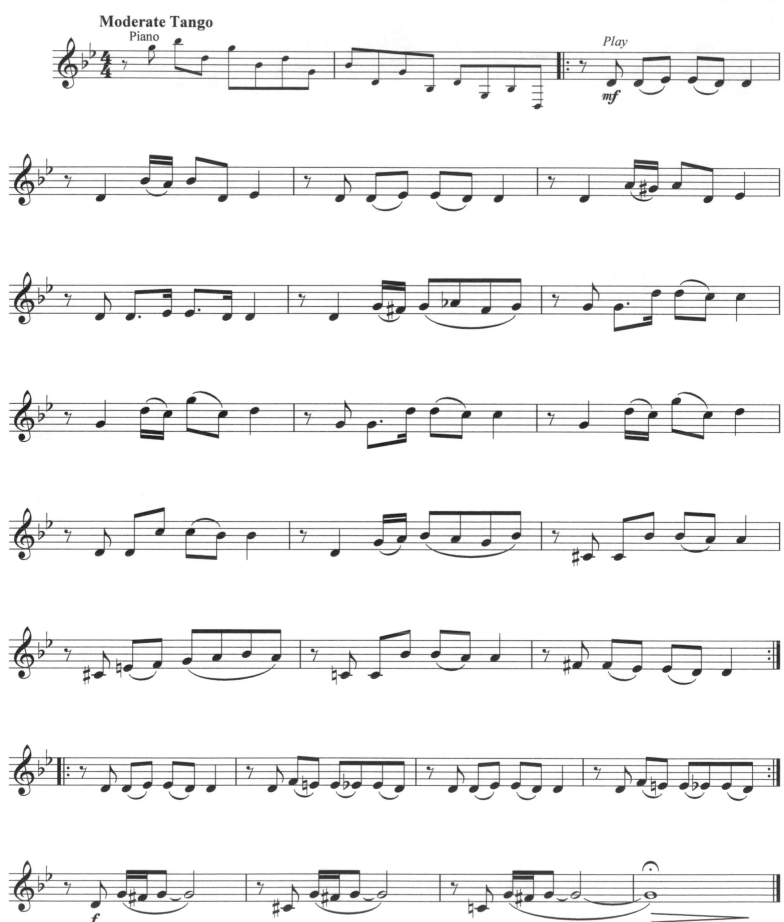

VUELVO AL SUR
(I'm Returning South)

CLARINET

ASTOR PIAZZOLLA

SIN RUMBO
(Aimless)

CLARINET

ASTOR PIAZZOLLA

19

STREET TANGO

CLARINET

ASTOR PIAZZOLLA

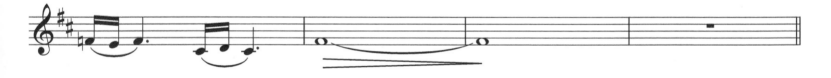

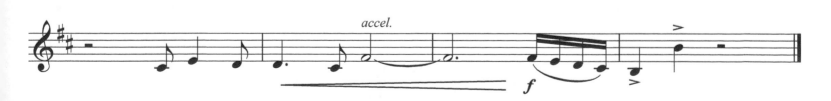

TANGO FINAL

from FAMILLE D'ARTISTES

CLARINET

ASTOR PIAZZOLLA